CONTINENTS

South America

Michael and Jane Pelusey

CHELSEA HOUSE
PUBLISHERS

A Haights Cross Communications Company

Philadelphia

This edition first published in 2005 in the United States of America by Chelsea House Publishers, a subsidiary of Haights Cross Communications.

Chelsea House Publishers
2080 Cabot Blvd West, Suite 201
Langhorne, PA 19047-1813

The Chelsea House world wide web address is www.chelseahouse.com

First published in 2004 by
MACMILLAN EDUCATION AUSTRALIA PTY LTD
627 Chapel Street, South Yarra 3141

Visit our website at www.macmillan.com.au

Associated companies and representatives throughout the world.

Copyright © Michael and Jane Pelusey 2004

Library of Congress Cataloging-in-Publication Data
Pelusey, Michael.
    South America / by Michael and Jane Pelusey.
    p. cm. – (Continents)
    Includes index.
    ISBN 0-7910-8277-6
    1. South America – Juvenile literature. I. Pelusey, Jane. II. Title.
    F2208.5.P45 2004
    980–dc22

                                                        2004015819

Edited by Angelique Campbell-Muir
Text design by Karen Young
Cover design by Karen Young
Illustrations by Nina Sanadze
Maps by Laurie Whiddon, Map Illustrations

Printed in China

Acknowledgements

The authors and the publisher are grateful to the following for permission to reproduce copyright material:

Cover photographs: El Condor in Tierra del Fuego, Chile, and macaw parrot, courtesy of Pelusey Photography.

All photographs © Pelusey Photography except for Artville, pp. 22 (bottom right), 24 (top); Corbis Digital Stock, p. 20 (bottom left); Digital Vision, p. 22 (bottom left); Imageaddict, p. 24 (center); Photodisc, pp. 20 (bottom right, top), 24 (bottom), 26 (bottom left); Stockbyte, pp. 22 (top), 26 (bottom right, top).

While every care has been taken to trace and acknowledge copyright, the publisher tenders their apologies for any accidental infringement where copyright has proved untraceable. Where the attempt has been unsuccessful, the publisher welcomes information that would redress the situation.

Please note

At the time of printing, the Internet addresses appearing in this book were correct. Owing to the dynamic nature of the Internet, however, we cannot guarantee that all these addresses will remain correct.

Contents

Glossary words

When a word is printed in **bold**, you can look up its meaning in the Glossary on page 31.

South America is a continent

South America is the fourth largest continent in the world. Look at a world map or globe and you can see that the world is made up of water and land. The big areas of land are called continents. There are seven continents:

- Africa
- Antarctica
- Asia
- Australia
- Europe
- North America
- South America.

Borders

The borders of continents follow natural physical features such as coastlines and mountain ranges. Most of South America's borders are oceans:

- Pacific Ocean
- Atlantic Ocean.

South America joins North America on a land border between the countries of Colombia and Panama.

World map showing the seven modern-day continents

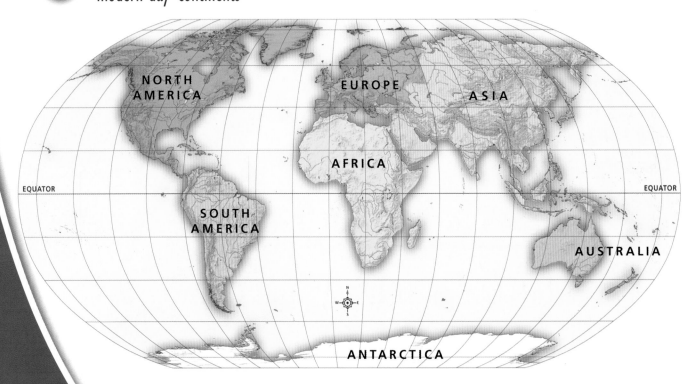

NORTH AMERICA

EUROPE

ASIA

AFRICA

EQUATOR

SOUTH AMERICA

AUSTRALIA

ANTARCTICA

EQUATOR

The world is a jigsaw

The Earth's crust is made up of huge plates, called **tectonic plates**, which fit together like a jigsaw puzzle. These plates are constantly moving, up and down and sideways, up to 4 inches (10 centimeters) a year. Over long periods of time, the plates change in size and shape as their edges push against each other.

Around 250 million years ago, there was one massive supercontinent called Pangaea. Around 200 million years ago, it began splitting and formed two continents. Laurasia was the northern continent and Gondwana was the southern continent. By about 65 million years ago, Laurasia and Gondwana had separated into smaller landmasses that look much like the continents we know today. Laurasia split to form Europe, Asia, and North America. Gondwana split to form South America, Africa, Australia, and Antarctica.

South America was once part of the supercontinent Pangaea.

The South American continent formed when Gondwana split into smaller landmasses.

Early South America

When the continents were one, animals moved across the land, as there was no water to stop them. When the continents split apart, the animals were left on separate landmasses and they began to change and develop into the animals we know today. During this time, dinosaurs roamed the Earth, including South America. As dinosaurs became **extinct**, other animals replaced them. The macrauchenia had a small trunk like an elephant, a body like a camel, and feet like a rhinoceros. The 20-foot- (6-meter-) long giant sloth had large back legs and moved slowly along the ground eating grass.

Early humans

Scientists believe modern humans, or *Homo sapiens*, came from Africa then made their way to Asia, and across to North America around 15,000 years ago. These people gradually moved into South America.

The macrauchenia lived in South America around 5 million years ago.

First civilizations

The first people of South America were called Amerindians. They moved to areas all over the continent. The Amerindians moved together to help each other grow crops and for protection. Some lived in the dense **tropical rain forests**, while others lived in the cold south with only fire to keep them warm. The first South American civilization was the Chavin Amerindians, who lived between 2,000 and 3,000 years ago. They lived in villages around **pyramids** built of stone and made pottery. Other Amerindians lived in tribes or smaller groups and developed their own **traditions**.

 The great Inca city of Machu Picchu was built high in the mountains.

An advanced South American civilization

Around 800 years ago, a group of people called the Incas developed an advanced civilization. They had great building and farming skills. The Incas pleased their gods by sacrificing or killing animals and people.

South America today

The physical features of the South American continent

South America covers an area of 6.8 million square miles (17.8 million square kilometers). There are 12 countries in South America. The biggest country is Brazil, which is 3,286,470 square miles (8,511,965 square kilometers) in size. Suriname is the smallest country at only 63,038 square miles (163,270 square kilometers).

Rio de Janeiro is a major city in Brazil.

Big country

Brazil is the fifth biggest country in the world and takes up about half of South America. Half of all South American people live in Brazil.

Physical features

The continent of South America is situated mainly in the **Southern Hemisphere**. The widest part of the continent is near the **equator**. Near the west coast of South America is a chain of high mountains. The mountains are capped in snow with glaciers or rivers of ice that flow off them. West of these mountains is a region of very dry desert. There are large flat areas called plains on the other side of these mountains. This region features hilly and low-lying swamps with huge rivers weaving through the rain forest. The southern tip of South America is mountainous and ends in a series of rugged islands.

South American people

South Americans come from many places around the world. Today, the people of South America are mostly a mix of Amerindians and people from countries such as Spain and Portugal.

The Andes Mountains in South America are the longest mountain range in the world.

This village is situated on the banks of the Amazon River in Brazil.

The land

South America is a land of many different features.

Mountains

The Andes Mountains are the longest mountain range in the world. They run down the western edge of South America. Cerro Aconcagua in Argentina at 22,833 feet (6,959 meters) is their highest peak. Many mountains in the Andes are volcanoes that sometimes erupt. The Guiana Highlands, in the north of South America, are flat-topped mountains known as plateaus. Great waterfalls tumble off these plateaus in Venezuela.

Deserts

The Atacama Desert lies west of the Andes Mountains. It is one of the driest places on Earth.

Plains

The Amazon Basin, a flat plain in Brazil, is an area nearly as big as the United States. Farther south in Argentina, these plains are called pampas and are mainly grasslands.

 This part of the Andes Mountains is in Tierra del Fuego, Argentina.

Rivers

The Amazon River begins in the Andes and flows right across the continent through Peru and Brazil. Many people live along its banks and use the river for transportation and fishing.

Lakes

Lake Titicaca is located in the Andes Mountains. It is the highest **navigable** lake in the world at 12,500 feet (3,810 meters) above sea level. Thick mats of floating plants cover parts of the lake. They are strong enough for people to live on them.

Big river facts

The Amazon River is the second longest river in the world at 4,050 miles (6,516 kilometers). The Nile River in Africa is the longest river.

The Amazon River is wide enough for huge cargo ships to sail through it.

Highest waterfall

Angel Falls in Venezuela is the highest waterfall in the world. The water falls 3,213 feet (979 meters).

This farmland is on an island in Lake Titicaca.

The climate

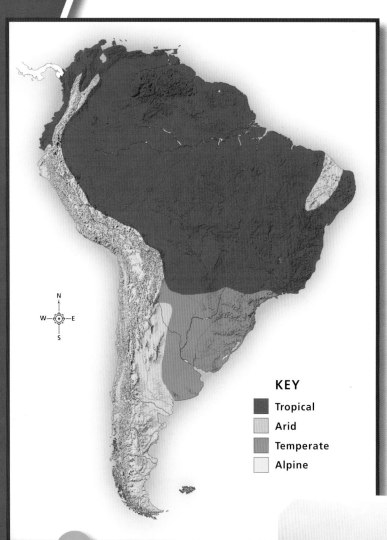

S outh America covers such a large area that it has many different climate zones. The main climates in South America are **tropical**, **temperate**, **alpine**, and **arid**.

Tropical

The tropical regions of South America are located around the equator. The temperatures are hot with high **humidity**. It rains heavily nearly every day so the Amazon River rises and often floods the surrounding rain forest. In dry spells the water level drops. Farther away from the equator, South America gets two seasons, the hot wet and the hot dry.

KEY

- Tropical
- Arid
- Temperate
- Alpine

Climate zones in South America

Storms are common in the Amazon River area.

Temperate

Outside the tropical zones, the eastern side of South America has a temperate climate with warm, humid summers and plenty of rain. Winters are cool and drier, especially in the south. Much of Argentina has a temperate climate.

Alpine

Most high peaks in the Andes Mountains are covered in snow and ice throughout the year. Temperatures can drop to 14 degrees Fahrenheit (−10 degrees Celsius) in the highest parts. Storms or blizzards bring snow and strong winds.

Arid

The deserts of South America have a very dry climate. Most of the Atacama Desert is made up of only sand and rock. In some places, rivers flowing from melting snow in the Andes pass through the desert. In these places, the land is green with plants grown by people.

The wettest place

The wettest place in South America is Quibdo in the Andes Mountains, Colombia. It gets 354 inches (8,991 millimeters) of rain a year.

The Atacama Desert meets the sea at the fishing port of Iquique.

 Many houses in Arica do not even need roofs.

The world's driest place

The Atacama Desert in Chile is one of the driest deserts in the world. The city of Arica gets less than 0.1 inches (2 millimeters) of rain a year. Often it does not rain for years.

Plants and animals

A macaw parrot

Giant tropical snails live in the Amazon Basin.

The biggest area of rain forest in the world is the Amazon Basin. Many Amazonian plants and animals are found nowhere else in the world.

Rain forest

Tall trees grow in the rain forest and smaller plants such as ferns and palms grow in the shade below.

Colorful parrots such as macaws fly among the tree branches looking for fruit to eat. Spotted cats called jaguars roam the forest floor hunting for animals such as wild pigs. The giant tropical snail is bigger than a man's hand.

The Amazon Basin is also home to millions of insects. Huge swarms of soldier ants march through the forest eating any creature that gets in their way.

Big fish

The Amazon River is home to one of the world's biggest freshwater fish. The arapaima can grow to 14 feet (4.5 meters) in length and weigh up to 440 pounds (200 kilograms).

 The guanaco is native to Chile.

Grasslands

The plains in the southern part of South America are covered in grasses. The llama, alpaca, and guanaco, all grass-eating animals related to the camel, live in these plains. They have long necks and soft hooves. People often use their wool for knitting and weaving.

Mountains

The guanaco also lives in the mountainous parts of Chile. It is hunted and eaten by a large cat called the puma.

Desert

Nothing can survive in the Atacama Desert. The seas off the desert coastline have millions of fish, which attract seabirds that nest on rocks along the coastline.

The Andean condor is the world's biggest flying bird.

Worlds' biggest flying bird

The Andean condor is a type of vulture that is found in the southern part of the Andes Mountains. It has a 10-foot (3-meter) wingspan and weighs up to 30 pounds (13.6 kilograms). Condors are scavengers, so they eat dead animals.

The people

This Amerindian woman lives in an Andean mountain village. She is spinning wool to make clothes.

South America is home to thousands of ethnic groups or tribes. Each group has its own traditions, beliefs, and languages.

Ethnic groups

The original South American people were Amerindians. They lived in different tribes or groups throughout South America. They hunted and fished in rain forest areas where there was plenty to eat. During the 1400s, the Spanish and the Portuguese discovered South America. Later, other people came from Europe. Argentina also has some people of Italian and German heritage. The main ethnic group in South America today is a mix of Amerindians and Spanish, called mestizos.

People facts	
Population	345 million people
Most populated country	Brazil with 180 million people
Least populated country	Suriname with 445,506 people

Languages

When the Spanish came to South America they brought with them their language. Spanish is the official language of most South American countries. Other European countries **colonized** places in the northeast part of the continent. The Portuguese ruled Brazil for many years, so Brazilians speak Portuguese. The people of Guyana speak English. Dutch is the official language of Suriname. Amerindian people also have their own traditional languages.

Religion

When the Europeans colonized South America they also brought the Christian religion with them. **Missionaries** converted many Amerindian people to Christianity. Today most South Americans are Catholic, a form of Christianity. Christians believe in one God and follow the teachings of Jesus, who they believe is the son of God. Some tribes have combined Christianity with their own traditional beliefs.

A Christian church in Bolivia

The virgin of Quito in Ecuador is a statue of Jesus's mother, Mary.

The countries

South American regions and countries

There are 12 countries in South America. The continent can be divided into the following regions:

- the North
- the South
- the East
- the West.

The South American countries that we know today did not exist 600 years ago, as the land belonged to different South American tribes. European people made the modern-day country borders within South America.

Colonies

When the Europeans colonized South America they took land away from the Amerindians. The Europeans also brought with them diseases such as measles. The Amerindians had no defense against these new diseases and many of them died.

Gaining independence

The Spanish South American countries became **independent** in the early 1800s. Brazil became independent from Portugal in 1822. The British ruled Guyana until 1966 and the Netherlands ruled Suriname until 1975. French Guiana is still a French colony.

An example of Spanish architecture built on top of Inca stonework in Cuzco, Peru

Fighting for land and freedom

Since South American countries became independent, their people have been involved in war and fighting. This fighting is often about Amerindians trying to get their land back from the government of their country. Other wars have started when a country has been taken over by a cruel leader. Over time, people become tired of being mistreated so they rise up and protest against the government. If the government is then overthrown, the uprising is called a coup (pronounced *coo*). Many South American governments have been removed by coups.

 Soldiers marching along a city street in Chile as part of a military parade

The North

There are five countries in the North of South America. Use the key below to find out about and compare each country's languages, religions, ethnic groups, agriculture, and natural resources.

Country	Languages	Religions	Ethnic groups	Agriculture	Natural resources
Colombia	■	✝	🧍 🧍 🧍 🧍 🧍	✳✿❖□	🔴◆◆◆◆◆◆◆◆◆◆◆◆
Ecuador	■ ■	✝	🧍 🧍 🧍	✿✳❖□☆✪	🔴◆◆◆
Guyana	■ ■ ■ ■	✝ ✿ ☾ ✩	🧍 🧍 🧍	□❖✿☆✪	◆◆◆
Suriname	■ ■ ■ ■ ■ ■	✝ ✿ ☾ ✩	🧍 🧍 🧍 🧍 🧍 🧍	❖✿✳☆	◆◆◆◆
Venezuela	■ ■	✝	🧍 🧍 🧍	❖□✿✳☆✪	🔴◆◆◆◆◆

Key	Languages	Religions	Ethnic groups	Agriculture	Natural resources
	■ Creole	✝ Christianity	🧍 African–American	❖ Cereal grains	◆ Bauxite or alumina
	■ Dutch	✿ **Hinduism**	🧍 Native American	✳ Coffee	◆ Coal
	■ English	☾ **Islam**	🧍 Asian	✪ Dairy	◆ Copper
	■ French	✩ Traditional beliefs	🧍 Creole or Mulatto	✿ Fruit and vegetables	◆ Diamonds
	■ Hindi		🧍 East Indian	✳ Peanuts	◆ Emeralds
	■ Spanish		🧍 European	☆ Sheep, cattle, and goats	◆ Gold
	■ Traditional languages		🧍 Mestizo	□ Sugar cane	◆ **Hydropower**
			🧍 Spanish		◆ Iron ore
					◆ Nickel
					🔴 Oil and gas
					◆ Timber

Venezuela in focus

Official name: Bolivarian Republic of Venezuela

Area: 352,142 square miles (912,050 square kilometers)

Population: 25 million

Capital: Caracas

Major cities: Valencia, Maracaibo, Puerto La Cruz

Colonial rule: Spain

Famous landmarks: Angel Falls

Famous people: Simón Bolívar (freedom fighter), Teresa Carreño (pianist)

Traditions: quinceanera (a big birthday party for 15-year-old Venezuelan girls)

Traditional food: comida criolla (pancakes), soups and stews with chicken, pork, or beef

Venezuela is in the tropical region of South America. The Guiana Highlands rise high above low plains covered in tropical rain forest. From these highlands waterfalls plunge into rivers that flow to the coast. The Orinoco River divides the country in half and is the longest river in Venezuela.

A waterfall plunges off the Guiana Highlands.

Ecuador in focus

Official name: Republic of Ecuador

Area: 109,483 square miles (283,560 square kilometers)

Population: 13 million

Capital: Quito

Major cities: Guayaquil, Cuenca, Ambato, Portoviejo

Colonial rule: Spain

Famous landmarks: Andes Mountains, Cotopaxi Volcano, Monastery of San Francisco in Quito

Famous people: Antonio José de Sucre (freedom fighter)

Traditions: Panama hats (taken by gold prospectors to Panama), Andean music

Traditional food: roasted guinea pig, soups, stews, tostadas de maiz (corn pancakes)

Ecuador is a mountainous country mostly set in the Andes Mountains where people bundle up against the cold. In the east of the country near Peru, the land drops steeply to the edge of the Amazon Basin. This part of Ecuador is hot and wet with dense rain forests.

Locals shop at a busy market in Quito, Ecuador.

The East

There are three countries in the East of South America. Use the key below to find out about and compare each country's languages, religions, ethnic groups, agriculture, and natural resources.

Country	Languages	Religions	Ethnic groups	Agriculture	Natural resources
Brazil	■ ■ ■ ■	✟	👤 👤 👤 👤	✻❖❑✢❂☆	◆◆◆◆◆◆◆◆◆◆
Paraguay	■ ■	✟	👤 👤	❑◎❖✢☆❂	◆◆◆
Uruguay	■	✟✡	👤 👤 👤	❖☆	◆

Key	Languages	Religions	Ethnic groups	Agriculture	Natural resources
	■ English	✟ Christianity	👤 African–American	❖ Cereal grains	◆ Bauxite or alumina
	▪ Portuguese	✡ **Judaism**	👤 Native American	❂ Citrus	◆ Gold
	▪ Spanish		👤 Creole or Mulatto	✻ Coffee	◆ Hydropower
	■ Traditional languages		👤 European	◎ Cotton	◆ Iron ore
			👤 Mestizo	❂ Dairy	◆ Nickel
				✢ Fruit and vegetables	● Oil and gas
				☆ Sheep, cattle, and goats	◆ Phosphates
				❑ Sugar cane	◆ Timber
					◆ Tin
					◆ Uranium

Brazil in focus

Official name: Federative Republic of Brazil

Area: 3,286,470 square miles
(8,511,965 square kilometers)

Population: 180 million

Capital: Brasília

Major cities: Rio de Janeiro, São Paulo, Goiania,
Recife, Salvador, Curitiba, Porto Alegre

Colonial rule: Portugal

Famous landmarks: Amazon River, Iguaçú Falls,
Christ the Redeemer Statue, and Sugarloaf Mountain
in Rio de Janeiro

Famous people: Pele (soccer player), Carlos Drummond
de Andrade (writer), Carmen Miranda (dancer and actor)

Traditions: Brazilian carnivals just before Easter, samba dancing,
futebol (soccer)

Traditional food: beef with rice and Brazilian black beans

Brazil is the largest country in South America. The Amazon River and the
surrounding rain forest cover much of the land. Much of the rain forest is
being cleared for farmland and timber.

The beaches in Rio de Janeiro are popular with locals and tourists.

Paraguay in focus

Official name: Republic of Paraguay

Area: 157,046 square miles (406,750 square kilometers)

Population: 6 million

Capital: Asunción

Major cities: Encarnación, Concepción

Colonial rule: Spain

Famous landmarks: Chaco District

Famous people: General Alfredo Stroessner
(political leader)

Traditions: lace making, bottle dance (dancing with a
bottle on your head)

Traditional food: chipas (corn bread), soyo (meat and
vegetable soup)

Paraguay is a mainly flat land. The Paraguay River flows
through the country from north to south. West of the river are
the swamps of the vast Chaco district. Toward Bolivia the land
becomes drier and hillier. East of the Paraguay River the land
rises to a plateau where there are rain forests.

A boy earns money by polishing shoes in a park in Asunción.

The South

There are two countries in the South of South America. Use the key below to find out about and compare each country's languages, religions, ethnic groups, agriculture, and natural resources.

Country	Languages	Religions	Ethnic groups	Agriculture	Natural resources
Argentina	■ ■ ■ ■ ■	✞ ✡	🧍 🧍 🧍	❖ ♣ ❊ ❀ ☆	◆ ◆ ◆ ◆ ◆ ◉ ◆
Chile	■	✞	🧍 🧍	❖ ❧ ❑ ♣ ☆	◆ ◆ ◆ ◆

Key	Languages	Religions	Ethnic groups	Agriculture	Natural resources
	■ English	✞ Christianity	🧍 Native American	❖ Cereal grains	◆ Copper
	■ French	✡ Judaism	🧍 European	♣ Fruit and vegetables	◆ Hydropower
	■ German		🧍 Mestizo	❊ Peanuts	◆ Iron ore
	■ Italian			☆ Sheep, cattle, and goats	◆ Lead
	■ Spanish			❑ Sugar beets	◉ Oil and gas
				❀ Tea	◆ Timber
				❧ Wine	◆ Tin
					◆ Uranium
					◆ Zinc

Argentina in focus

Many Italians live in the Boca District of Buenos Aires.

Official name: Argentine Republic

Area: 1,068,296 square miles (2,766,890 square kilometers)

Population: 37 million

Capital: Buenos Aires

Major cities: Rosario, Mendosa, Salta, Comodora Rivadavia Ushuaia

Colonial rule: Spain

Famous landmarks: Cerro Aconcagua (South America's highest mountain), Iguaçú Falls (widest waterfall in the world)

Famous people: Juan and Eva Perón (political leaders), Diego Maradona (soccer player), Che Guevara (freedom fighter)

Traditions: gauchos (Argentine cowboys), tango (a dance)

Traditional food: beef with rice and potatoes

Argentina is mountainous in the west where the Andes are located. The southern tip of Argentina is a cold rugged island called Tierra del Fuego (owned by both Argentina and Chile). Most of the country is covered in grasslands, an area known as Patagonia, which is used to graze cattle and sheep.

Chile in focus

Official name: Republic of Chile

Area: 292,258 square miles (756,950 square kilometers)

Population: 15 million

Capital: Santiago

Major cities: Arica, Iguigue, Antofagasta, Concepción, Puerto Montt, Valparaiso

Colonial rule: Spain

Famous landmarks: Torres del Paine (Towers of Granite), Atacama Desert

Famous people: General Augusto Pinochet and Salvador Allende (political leaders), Isabel Allende (writer)

Traditions: rodeos on Independence Day

Traditional food: cazuke de ave (chicken and potato stew), empanada (meat pastie), eel is the national dish

Torres del Paine is at the southern tip of the Andes Mountains.

Chile is a long thin country of mainly deserts and mountains. The Atacama Desert in the north almost never gets rain. The snowcapped Andes Mountains run down the eastern side of Chile. Near the capital city of Santiago there are farms and wineries.

The West

There are two countries in the West of South America. Use the key below to find out about and compare each country's languages, religions, ethnic groups, agriculture, and natural resources.

Country	Languages	Religions	Ethnic groups	Agriculture	Natural resources
Bolivia	■ ■	✝ ☼	👤 👤 👤	❖ ✳ ♣ ◎ ❏	◆ ● ◆ ◆ ◆ ◆ ◆ ◆ ◆
Peru	■ ■	✝ ☼	👤 👤 👤 👤	✳ ◎ ❏ ❖ ♣ ☆ ✪	◆ ◆ ◆ ● ◆ ◆ ◆ ◆ ◆

Key	Languages	Religions	Ethnic groups	Agriculture	Natural resources
	■ Spanish	✝ Christianity	👤 African–American	❖ Cereal grains	◆ Coal
	■ Traditional languages	☼ Traditional beliefs	👤 Native American	✳ Coffee	◆ Copper
			👤 European	◎ Cotton	◆ Gold
			👤 Mestizo	✪ Dairy	◆ Hydropower
				♣ Fruit and vegetables	◆ Iron ore
				☆ Sheep, cattle, and goats	◆ Lead
				❏ Sugar cane	● Oil and gas
					◆ Phosphates
					◆ Silver
					◆ Timber
					◆ Tin
					◆ Zinc

Peru in focus

Cuzco was originally an Inca city.

Official name: Republic of Peru

Area: 496,223 square miles
(1,285,220 square kilometers)

Population: 28 million

Capital: Lima

Major cities: Iquitos, Cuzco, Trujillo, Arequipa

Colonial rule: Spain

Famous landmarks: Machu Picchu, Lake Titicaca

Famous people: Javier Perez de Cuellar
(past leader of the United Nations)

Traditions: Andean music such as pan pipes

Traditional food: ceviche de corvina (raw fish soaked in lemon juice)

Peru is one of the Andean countries. Many people live in the high mountain areas. These mountains are very rugged and cold, making life for the people very tough. Not all of Peru is mountainous. West of the Andes the land drops to a narrow coastal area. East of the Andes the climate becomes hot and wet as the land drops to the edge of the Amazon Basin.

Bolivia in focus

The Bolivian Alto Plano, or High Plain

Official name: Republic of Bolivia

Area: 424,161 square miles
(1,098,580 square kilometers)

Population: 9 million

Capital: La Paz and Sucre

Major cities: Santa Cruz, Potosi

Colonial rule: Spain

Famous landmarks: Lake Titicaca

Famous people: Franz Tamayo (poet),
Guzmán de Rojas (painter)

Traditions: Andean music such as pan pipes

Traditional food: saltenas (meat stew in dough), hot chili

Most of Bolivia is located in the Andes Mountains and high plains called the Alto Plano. La Paz in Bolivia is the highest capital city in the world. The city is situated at 11,929 feet (3,636 meters) above sea level.

South America's future

The future of South America is aimed at looking after the environment and improving the health and education of its people. The main problems are overcrowded cities and uncontrolled clearing of rain forests.

A flavella in Rio de Janeiro

Challenges

To find work, many South American people are leaving their farms and moving to the big cities. Without jobs, though, they are forced to live in tin shacks they make themselves. In Brazil these areas are called flavellas. With all these new people coming in from the country, cities in South America are growing very fast. Nearly 30 million people live in São Paulo and Rio de Janeiro in Brazil alone. The main challenge for the governments of South America is to find jobs for these people so they can have better lives.

Goals

The main goal for South American people is to provide good education and healthy lives for their children. In the future, South Americans intend to use more of their natural resources and industries to provide work for their children.

South Americans want to be able to provide better lives for their children.

Rain forest clearing

The Amazon rain forest is sometimes called the lungs of the Earth. The rain forest is the size of the United States and produces a lot of the oxygen we breathe. Every day, huge areas of forest are cleared for farmland and timber. Governments and scientists in South America are finding ways to slow this land clearing so the rain forest can grow back.

Medicine

Rain forests are the home of many rare types of animals and plants. Some lifesaving drugs have been created from rain forest plants. The goal is for scientists to find more cures by testing more plants. They believe it is possible that a cure for cancer could be found in this way.

South America in review

South America is the fourth smallest continent.

Area: 6.8 million square miles
(17.8 million square kilometers)

Population: 345 million

**First humans in
South America:** 15,000 years ago

First civilizations: Chavin
Amerindians 3,000 years ago

Other civilizations: Incas

Countries: 12

Biggest country: Brazil

Smallest country: Suriname

Most crowded country: Ecuador

Highest point: Cerro Aconcagua at 22,833 feet (6,959 meters)

Longest river: Amazon River in Brazil at 4,050 miles (6,516 kilometers)

Climate zones: tropical, temperate, alpine, arid

South American regions: the North, the South, the East, the West

Most common languages: Spanish, Portuguese, English, Dutch,
traditional languages

Web sites

For more information on South America go to:
http://www.fluid7.demon.co.uk/adventures/home.htm
http://www.mrdowling.com/712southamerica.html
http://www.worldatlas.com/webimage/countrys/sa.htm

Glossary

alpine a cold, snowy climate in high mountainous regions

arid a dry, desert-like climate

colonized when one country takes over another country

equator an imaginary line around the middle of the Earth's surface

extinct when no more of a particular species of animal or plant are left on the Earth

Hinduism an Indian religion that worships one God through many statues called deities

humidity the amount of water vapor in the air

hydropower power made by fast-flowing water

independent when a country governs itself

Islam a religion that believes in one God called Allah and the messages God gave to Muhammed

Judaism a religion that believes in one God and follows the teachings in the holy book called the Torah

missionaries people who travel to other countries to convert the local people to Christianity

navigable able to be traveled by ship

pyramids four-sided buildings with triangular sides meeting at a single point at the top

Southern Hemisphere the half of the Earth south of the equator

tectonic plates large pieces of the Earth's crust that move slowly, causing earthquakes

temperate a mild climate with wet weather and cool temperatures

traditions the way something has been done for many years

tropical a hot, humid, and wet climate found near the equator

tropical rain forests areas dense with tall trees and undergrowth found in hot, wet climates

Index